Corfu

Travel Guide 2024

A Journey through Time, Culture, and Coastal Beauty in 2024/2025

Ralph L. Hooley

Copyright © 2024 by Ralph L. Hooley

Disclaimer

The information provided in this travel guide is for general informational purposes only. While every effort has been made to ensure the accuracy of the content, the author and publisher cannot be held responsible for any errors or omissions. Travelers are encouraged to verify information independently and use their discretion when planning and undertaking activities.

Content

Introduction

Welcome to Corfu

Greetings, fellow adventurers! Step into the allure of Corfu, a captivating gem nestled in the heart of the Ionian Sea. In this guide, envision a journey beyond the ordinary, where each cobblestone street whispers tales of the past, and sun-kissed beaches beckon you to revel in the beauty of the present.

Corfu is not just a destination; it's a rich tapestry woven with threads of history, cultural diversity, and landscapes ranging from olive groves to turquoise shores. Picture Venetian fortresses overseeing bustling markets, the aroma of traditional Greek cuisine wafting through the air, and azure waters inviting you to relax along sandy shores.

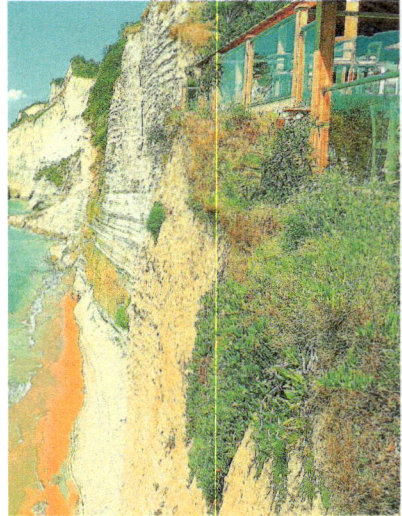

What distinguishes Corfu is the tangible sense of timelessness. From the narrow alleys of Corfu Town to the panoramic views of Paleokastritsa, each corner narrates a story of resilience, heritage, and the warm embrace of its people.

Corfu seamlessly blends tradition with modernity, offering a spectrum of experiences for every traveler. Whether you crave outdoor adventures, the tranquility of historical landmarks, or the lively atmosphere of local festivals, Corfu unfolds as a canvas of possibilities.

In your 2024 exploration, let this guide be your compass through hidden gems and well-trodden paths, revealing the unique charm that defines Corfu. Allow the spirit of adventure to lead you, creating moments of discovery, connection, and the enchantment only this island can provide.

Prepare to absorb the essence of Corfu – where history meets hospitality, and every sunset paints a new chapter in your travel tale.

Kalos irthate stin Kerkira! (Welcome to Corfu!)

What's New in 2024

Corfu, a dynamic destination pulsating with life, invites you to a year filled with exciting transformations, events, and attractions. In 2024, the island offers both returning and new visitors an array of fresh experiences. Let's delve into what makes Corfu an essential destination this year.

Discovering Unseen Gems

- Beyond its renowned landmarks, Corfu's allure lies in hidden gems waiting to be unearthed. In 2024, the island introduces new pathways, unveiling pockets of beauty, from charming villages to secluded beaches. Prepare to stray from the well-trodden routes and reveal the authentic essence of Corfu.

A Tapestry of Culture

- Immerse yourself in a vibrant cultural tapestry woven with festivals, exhibitions, and events. In 2024, Corfu bursts with life through a calendar of celebrations spotlighting the island's artistic, culinary, and musical talents. Traditional folk festivals and contemporary art exhibitions offer something for every taste and interest.

Gastronomic Adventures

- Corfu's culinary scene takes the spotlight with inventive gastronomic experiences. Emerging chefs and local establishments collaborate to craft culinary journeys fusing tradition with modern flair. Whether you're a seasoned food enthusiast or a casual diner, 2024 presents a feast of flavors to tantalize your taste buds.

Sustainability at the Forefront

- Dedicated to preserving its natural beauty and cultural heritage, Corfu introduces sustainable tourism initiatives in 2024. Visitors are encouraged to engage in eco-friendly practices, from beach clean-up events to initiatives promoting responsible tourism. Contribute to the conservation of Corfu's pristine environment during your visit.

Modernized Infrastructure

- To elevate your travel experience, Corfu invests in modern infrastructure. Enhanced transportation options, upgraded amenities, and improved accessibility streamline your exploration of the island. Whether navigating historic streets or venturing into the countryside, these enhancements ensure a seamless and enjoyable journey.

Embark on your Corfu adventure in 2024, captivated by the island's evolution. Embrace the new, savor the timeless, and let the spirit of discovery guide you through Corfu's ever-evolving landscape.

Quick Guide to Corfu

Situated in the cradle of the Ionian Sea, Corfu entices with a captivating blend of history, culture, and natural beauty. This guide is your key to unlocking the wonders of this island, a place where each moment unfolds like a chapter in an unforgettable adventure.

Location

- Corfu, also known as Kerkyra in Greek, lies off the northwest coast of mainland Greece. Its strategic position in the Ionian Sea has woven a tapestry of history shaped by the Venetians, French, British, and Greeks.

Climate

- Corfu basks in a Mediterranean climate, offering long, warm summers and mild, wet winters. Picture sun-soaked days where the azure sky kisses crystal-clear waters, providing a perfect setting for exploration. The island's lush landscapes owe their vibrancy to occasional rainfall, transforming Corfu into a verdant paradise.

Distinctive Features

Corfu is not merely an island; it's a diverse mosaic of landscapes and experiences waiting to be unveiled:

Corfu Town: The capital, a UNESCO World Heritage site, enchants with its blend of Venetian, French, and British architecture. Stroll through narrow alleys, explore historic fortresses, and immerse yourself in the vibrant atmosphere of Spianada Square.

Historical Landmarks: Corfu boasts an array of landmarks, including the Old and New Fortresses, the Liston Promenade, and the Achilleion Palace, each narrating tales that span centuries.

Natural Wonders: From the rugged allure of Mount Pantokrator to the panoramic views of the Angelokastro fortress, Corfu's natural wonders captivate the adventurous spirit. Discover hidden caves, traverse lush olive groves, and unwind on pristine beaches.

Culinary Delights: Corfu's cuisine mirrors its cultural influences, presenting a delectable fusion of Greek, Italian, and British flavors. Indulge in local specialties like Pastitsada, Sofrito, and an array of fresh seafood dishes.

Envision Corfu as more than a destination—a place where the past and present converge, creating an experience that transcends the ordinary. Explore the richness of this island as you navigate through these pages.

Getting Started

Travel Planning Tips

Best Time to Visit:
Corfu's Mediterranean climate makes it a year-round destination. Choose the season that suits your preferences:

Spring (April to June): Mild temperatures, blooming landscapes, and fewer crowds create an ideal exploration environment.

Summer (July to August): Peak tourist season with warm temperatures and lively vibes, perfect for beach enthusiasts.

Autumn (September to October): Enjoy pleasant weather, fewer tourists, and cultural exploration opportunities.

Winter (November to March): Experience Corfu's authentic charm away from crowds in mild, rainy weather.

Visa Requirements:
Ensure you have the necessary travel documents:

EU Citizens: No visa needed; a valid ID card or passport is sufficient for stays up to 90 days.

Non-EU Citizens: Check country-specific visa requirements, typically requiring a Schengen visa for up to 90 days.

Transportation:
Navigate Corfu's well-connected transportation network:

Getting Around: Utilize buses, taxis, or consider renting a car for flexibility beyond main towns.

Renting a Car: Ensure a valid driver's license; drive on the right side with Greek road signs.

Packing Essentials:
Pack strategically for various seasons:

Clothing: Light attire for summer, layers for cooler seasons, swimwear, comfortable shoes, and a light jacket.

Sun Protection: Shield yourself with sunscreen, sunglasses, and a hat during sunny days.

Adapters: Bring Type C and Type F electrical socket adapters for device charging.

Currency and Money Matters:
Understand financial aspects in Euro (EUR):

ATMs: Widely available in urban areas; carry cash for smaller establishments.

Credit Cards: Accepted in major places, but cash may be preferred in smaller businesses.

Currency Exchange: Available at banks with competitive rates.

Time Zone:
Corfu operates on Eastern European Time (EET) and Eastern European Summer Time (EEST) during Daylight Saving Time.

Language and Communication:

English is spoken in tourist areas; learn a few phrases:

Common Phrases: Kalimera, Kalispera, Efharisto, Parakalo, Ne (Yes) / Ohi (No).

Tipping: Customary in restaurants; round up the bill or leave a 5-10% tip.

Health and Safety:

Prioritize well-being with these considerations:

Healthcare: Modern facilities available; carry EHIC for EU citizens or comprehensive travel insurance.

Emergency Numbers: Medical Emergency (166), Police (100), Fire Department (199).

Safety: Corfu is generally safe; take standard precautions and be aware of surroundings.

Local Customs:

Enhance cultural experiences by respecting local customs:

Dress Modestly: Cover shoulders and knees when visiting churches or monasteries.

Greetings: Warmly greet locals with "Kalimera" or "Kalispera."

Socializing: Embrace Greek socializing; be open to conversations and invitations.

Electricity:
Corfu uses European standard sockets; bring appropriate adapters for 230V voltage, 50Hz frequency.

Packing Guide

Clothing Essentials

- **Light Attire**: Corfu's Mediterranean climate calls for light, breathable fabrics to keep you cool in the summer heat.

- **Swimwear**: Essential for basking in the sun on pristine beaches or discovering hidden coves. Don't forget your favorite swimsuit.

- **Versatile Layers**: Plan for cooler evenings by packing a light jacket or sweater. Versatile layers ensure comfort in varying temperatures.

- **Sturdy Walking Shoes**: Explore Corfu's charming streets and historical sites on foot with comfortable walking shoes.

- **Sun Protection Gear**: Shield yourself from the intense Mediterranean sun with a wide-brimmed hat and sunglasses.

Toiletries Must-Haves

- **High SPF Sunscreen**: Protect your skin during outdoor activities with a high SPF sunscreen.

- **Insect Repellent**: Especially crucial if venturing into nature trails or rural areas.

- **Compact Toiletry Kit**: Organize personal hygiene items and medications in a compact toiletry bag.

Miscellaneous Essentials

- **Compact Umbrella**: Be ready for occasional rain, particularly in the winter months.

- **Basic Greek Language Guide**: Enhance your interactions with locals by carrying a basic Greek language guide.

- **Travel Comfort Items**: Consider a travel pillow and blanket, especially for cooler months or longer journeys.

Beach Adventure Necessities

- **Compact Beach Towel**: While accommodations often provide towels, a lightweight beach towel can be handy.

- **Easy Slip-Ons**: Transition from sandy shores to your accommodation effortlessly with flip flops.

- **Personal Snorkeling Gear**: Dive into underwater exploration with your own snorkeling gear, if you're a fan.

Explore Corfu

Overview of Corfu

Corfu, an Ionian gem, exudes a timeless allure that transcends eras. Rich in history, adorned with natural splendor, and woven with a vibrant cultural fabric, Corfu stands as a captivating destination for the discerning traveler. Let's uncover the essence that makes Corfu an irresistible journey.

Landscapes

Corfu's panoramas unfold like chapters in a captivating story. Endless olive groves stretch across the horizon, punctuated by villages frozen in time. Stroll through narrow village streets, where houses adorned with bougainvillea evoke an enduring charm.

Venture further, and the scenery transforms into a canvas of azure seas and sun-kissed beaches. Corfu's coastline, a natural masterpiece, invites relaxation under the Mediterranean sun. From the dramatic cliffs of Paleokastritsa to Mount Pantokrator's panoramic vistas, the island's topography is a visual symphony.

Architecture

17

Corfu's architecture narrates a history shaped by Venetian, French, British, and Greek influences. Corfu Town, a UNESCO World Heritage site, unveils Venetian-inspired charm. The Liston Promenade, bordered by elegant arcades, offers a stroll through a bygone era.

Explore the Old and New Fortresses' stone corridors, where tales of resilience echo through the centuries. Navigate the Kanoni district's narrow alleys, presenting postcard-perfect scenes of houses overlooking azure waters.

Atmosphere

Corfu's ambiance blends laid-back island life with vibrant cultural vigor. Picture relishing a seaside meal, the scent of freshly caught seafood mingling with the salty breeze. Squares buzz with laughter, music, and clinking glasses, inviting you to embrace the convivial spirit of the locals.

Corfu seamlessly marries relaxation with exploration—be it exploring markets, sipping coffee in historic cafés, or joining lively festivals, a palpable joie de vivre fills the air.

Must-Visit Destinations

• **Corfu Town**: Immerse yourself in the enchanting maze of Corfu Town, where Spianada Square, Liston Promenade, and historic fortresses beckon exploration.

- **Paleokastritsa**: Discover the mesmerizing beauty of Paleokastritsa, where monasteries perch on cliffs overlooking the turquoise sea.

- **Kavos**: Nightlife enthusiasts find paradise in Kavos, with beach parties and entertainment lasting well into the night.

- **Kanoni**: Enjoy panoramic views of Mouse Island and Vlacherna Monastery in Kanoni, a district offering tranquility and charm.

Corfu's allure lies not only in its iconic landmarks but in serendipitous moments found in its hidden corners. A destination inviting you to embrace both the grandeur of its history and the simplicity of its daily life.

Historical Landmarks

Corfu unfolds its historical tapestry like a captivating tale, where each landmark whispers of the island's diverse past. For aficionados of history, Corfu is a repository of architectural wonders and sites that stand witness to centuries of influences. Let's embark on a journey through time and explore the historical landmarks shaping Corfu's cultural legacy.

Old Fortress (Palaio Frourio)

Approaching Corfu Town, the imposing silhouette of the Old Fortress commands attention. Erected on a rocky promontory in the 6th century, this fortress has guarded the island through Byzantine, Venetian, and British epochs. Wander through its gates, bastions, and tunnels, tracing the footsteps of conquerors. The summit offers panoramic views of Corfu Town and the Ionian Sea, connecting you with the island's maritime history.

New Fortress (Neo Frourio)

Built in the 16th century, the New Fortress complements the Old Fortress in safeguarding Corfu Town. With Venetian-inspired architecture, its battlements provide insight into Corfu's historical significance. The fortress houses the Church of St. George, a poignant reminder of the island's religious heritage.

Achilleion Palace

Perched on Gastouri's hills, Achilleion Palace is a testament to Empress Elisabeth of Bavaria's romantic vision. Built in the late 19th century, the palace immerses visitors in Greek mythology and imperial opulence. The palace gardens, adorned with sculptures and panoramic views, invite contemplation and admiration.

Liston Promenade

Inspired by Paris's Rue de Rivoli, Corfu's Liston Promenade radiates cosmopolitan charm. Constructed during French occupation, the esplanade's arched colonnades invite leisurely strolls and café culture. It stands as a testament to Corfu's cultural exchanges and a prime spot to absorb the island's unique atmosphere.

Angelokastro

Perched on the island's highest peak, Angelokastro transports visitors to a bygone era. Dating back to the Byzantine period, this fortress played a crucial role in protecting Corfu. The journey rewards explorers with panoramic views of the coastline, making it a must-visit for those seeking a historical and scenic adventure.

Mon Repos

Escape to the tranquility of Mon Repos, a neoclassical palace surrounded by lush gardens. Built in the 19th century, Mon Repos holds historical significance as the birthplace of Prince Philip, Duke of Edinburgh. Today, it stands as a serene retreat, inviting visitors to explore its grounds and the remnants of ancient structures that reveal Corfu's layers of history.

Spianada Square

At the heart of Corfu Town lies Spianada Square, one of Europe's largest squares. Surrounded by elegant buildings, it reflects the influence of the French occupation. The Liston Promenade, cricket matches, and the iconic Maitland Monument create an atmospheric gathering place, providing a glimpse into Corfu's social and cultural dynamics.

As you explore these historical landmarks, each step resonates with the echoes of empires, cultural exchanges, and the resilience of Corfu through the ages. Whether captivated by medieval fortresses or neoclassical palaces, Corfu's historical treasures offer a journey through time, inviting you to delve into the island's captivating narrative.

Natural Wonders

Corfu unveils its natural splendors in a captivating array of landscapes, enticing travelers to discover the island's unspoiled allure. From azure coastlines to lush hills, Corfu's natural treasures await exploration. Join us on a journey through the island's wonders, where picturesque parks, breathtaking viewpoints, and unique landscapes define Corfu's essence.

1. Paleokastritsa

Located on the northwest coast, Paleokastritsa is a celestial retreat capturing the imagination. Crowned by the 13th-century Paleokastritsa Monastery, this area features crystalline waters and lush greenery. Explore the Monastery's grounds, revealing panoramic views of the Ionian Sea, hidden caves, and secluded beaches, making Paleokastritsa a haven for nature enthusiasts.

2. Mount Pantokrator

As Corfu's highest peak, Mount Pantokrator invites adventurers to ascend its slopes for unparalleled views. A winding road or hiking trail leads to the summit, where a monastery dedicated to the Transfiguration of Christ awaits. The panoramic vista unveils Corfu's patchwork of landscapes, from olive groves to coastal panoramas.

3. Canal d'Amour

On the northern coast near Sidari, the Canal d'Amour, or the Channel of Love, is a natural wonder steeped in folklore. Couples who swim through this narrow channel, legend has it, will marry soon. Unique sandstone formations and crystal-clear waters add a touch of romance to this enchanting spot, a must-visit for those seeking beauty and mythology.

4. Angel's Trail

Nature enthusiasts can explore the Angel's Trail, a scenic hike unveiling Corfu's diverse ecosystems. Starting near Palaiokastritsa, the trail meanders through cypress forests, olive groves, and wildflower-strewn landscapes. The journey culminates at the summit of Angelokastro, offering breathtaking views of the coastline and surrounding islands.

5. Corfu Trail

For passionate trekkers, the Corfu Trail is a long-distance path spanning the island. Winding through diverse terrain, including olive groves, coastal cliffs, and traditional villages, the trail allows hikers to experience Corfu's natural beauty up close. Immerse yourself in the island's flora, fauna, and captivating scenery.

6. Kanoni and Mouse Island

Kanoni, with its iconic view of Mouse Island (Pontikonisi), presents a postcard-perfect scene. The Vlacherna Monastery, perched on a tiny islet connected by a causeway, adds serenity to the panoramic setting. Enjoy the view from elevated terraces, where azure waters, Mouse Island, and distant mountains create a picturesque tableau.

7. Corfu's Beaches

Corfu's coastline boasts a myriad of beaches, each with its unique charm. From the golden sands of Glyfada to the pebbled shores of Agios Gordios, the beaches offer a spectrum of experiences. Choose between lively beachfronts with water sports or secluded coves for a tranquil escape—Corfu's beaches cater to every preference.

8. Corfu Botanical Garden

Founded in 1984, the Corfu Botanical Garden is a verdant oasis showcasing the island's diverse flora. Located in the Kanoni area, the garden spans over 60 acres, featuring plant collections from Asia, Africa, and the Americas. Stroll through lush greenery, discover rare species, and enjoy the serene ambiance of this botanical haven.

Corfu's natural wonders weave a tapestry of colors, textures, and sensations, inviting you to explore the island's ecological diversity. Whether hiking mountain trails, unwinding on pristine beaches, or gazing upon panoramic vistas, Corfu's natural beauty is a testament to the island's enchanting allure.

Popular Beaches

Corfu, a jewel in the Ionian Sea, boasts a diverse coastline adorned with enchanting beaches. Let's embark on a journey to explore some of the island's finest seaside destinations, each with its unique charm.

Glyfada Beach

- **Character**: A crescent of golden sand embraced by verdant hills, Glyfada Beach is alive with activity. Shallow, clear waters beckon visitors seeking both relaxation and excitement.

- **Amenities**: Beachside tavernas offer delectable Greek cuisine, while water sports enthusiasts can indulge in activities like paragliding and jet-skiing. Well-equipped facilities ensure a full day of seaside enjoyment.

- **What Makes it Special**: The scenic beauty of Glyfada, coupled with its lively ambiance, makes it a favorite among both locals and tourists.

Paleokastritsa Beach

- **Character**: Nestled beneath the imposing Paleokastritsa Monastery, this beach boasts crystal-clear turquoise waters against a backdrop of rugged cliffs, creating a serene and picturesque setting.

- **Amenities**: Sunbeds and umbrellas are available, and boat trips offer exploration opportunities. Tavernas along the shoreline serve traditional Corfiot cuisine with stunning sea views.

- **What Makes it Special**: The combination of a pristine beach, historical monastery, and opportunities for exploration make Paleokastritsa a multifaceted destination.

Agios Gordios Beach

- **Character**: Tucked between dramatic cliffs, Agios Gordios Beach is a wide stretch of golden sand embraced by lush green hills, offering clear waters and a laid-back village atmosphere.

- **Amenities**: Well-equipped with sunbeds and umbrellas, the beach also caters to water sports enthusiasts with kayaking and paddleboarding. The village offers a variety of tavernas and beachfront bars.

- **What Makes it Special**: Agios Gordios blends natural beauty with a welcoming community atmosphere, making it a tranquil beach getaway.

Canal d'Amour Beach

- **Character**: Located near Sidari, Canal d'Amour is renowned for its unique sandstone formations and romantic legend. Sandy shores and shallow waters create a captivating and idyllic setting.

- **Amenities**: Sunbeds and umbrellas are available, and the nearby village offers a variety of dining options. Easily accessible, it's a popular choice for couples and families.

- **What Makes it Special**: The legend of Canal d'Amour adds enchantment to this beach, making it a favorite spot for romantic getaways.

Myrtiotissa Beach

- **Character**: Known as Corfu's "hidden gem," Myrtiotissa Beach is a secluded haven surrounded by cliffs and lush vegetation, offering golden sand and clear waters in an intimate setting.

Amenities: While maintaining a natural charm, the beach offers minimal facilities, allowing visitors to enjoy its unspoiled beauty. A taverna provides refreshments for those seeking a peaceful escape.

- **What Makes it Special**: Myrtiotissa's unspoiled beauty and secluded nature make it a retreat for those seeking a tranquil escape.

Kavos Beach

- **Character**: Situated at the southern tip, Kavos Beach is known for its lively atmosphere, long stretches of sand, and a variety of water sports. Beachfront bars contribute to its vibrant scene.

- **Amenities**: Abundant sunbeds, water sports facilities, and beach bars create a hub of entertainment, drawing in a younger crowd seeking a lively beach experience.

- **What Makes it Special**: Kavos is the go-to destination for a lively beach experience, combining sun, sea, and a vibrant nightlife scene popular among younger travelers.

Corfu's beaches promise diverse experiences, from serene retreats to lively coastal hubs, inviting visitors to explore the beauty of its captivating coastline. Next, let's delve into the various accommodation options, ensuring a comfortable and enjoyable stay on this picturesque island.

Accommodation

Hotels

Siora Vittoria Boutique Hotel

Arrival Details:

- Discover the hotel at Stefanou Padova 36, Ágios Rókkos, 491 00, Greece.

- Just a brief 10-minute stroll from Corfu Old Town and the nearest beach awaits.

- Accessible by taxi, bus, or car, your journey is effortlessly convenient.

- If landing at Corfu International Airport (CFU), choose between a 30-minute taxi ride (€20-€25) or a 45-minute bus ride (€1.50) to reach the hotel.

Insider Insights:

- Secure the best rates by booking directly through the hotel's website.

- For peak season travels (June-August), plan ahead to secure your room.

- Opt for a room with a balcony for breathtaking vistas of the Old Town and the sea.

- Don't miss the complimentary daily breakfast buffet in the garden.

- Enhance your exploration by renting a bike from the hotel to tour Corfu Town on two wheels.

- Consult the hotel staff for local recommendations on dining, drinking, and shopping in Corfu Town.

Operating Hours:

- Accessible 24/7, the hotel welcomes guests every day of the week.

Dining Details:

- Indulge in the hotel's restaurant, offering breakfast, lunch, and dinner.

- Enjoy a complimentary breakfast for most room types.

- Lunch and dinner options range from €15 to €30 per person.

Prime Location:

- Nestled in a tranquil and secure area of Corfu Town, the hotel is a short walk from key attractions – Old Town, beaches, and shops.

Security Assurance:

- Your safety is a priority with 24-hour security and a CCTV system.

- Each guest room is equipped with a safe deposit box.

Facilities and Amenities:

- Dive into the hotel's offerings, including a swimming pool, garden, sun terrace, restaurant, bar, lounge area, and business center.

- Additional perks feature free Wi-Fi, luggage storage, and laundry services for a seamless stay.

Corfu Palace

Arrival Options:

• **By Air**: Your journey begins at Corfu International Airport (CFU), just 3 km from the hotel. Conveniently reach the hotel via taxi, bus, or shuttle.

• **By Sea**: For a scenic route, ferries from Greek mainland ports and Italy dock at Corfu. The ferry terminal, only 1 km from the hotel, allows for a leisurely stroll or a quick taxi ride to your destination.

Operating Hours:

- Open 24/7, the Corfu Palace awaits your arrival at any time.

Dining Costs:

- Indulge in culinary delights at varying prices. Anticipate spending €20-€50 for breakfast, €30-€60 for lunch, and €50-€100 for dinner, depending on your chosen restaurant and dish.

Insider Recommendations:

- **Advance Booking**: Secure your room ahead, particularly during peak seasons (July-August).

- **Budget-Friendly Dining**: Explore affordable dining options nearby if you're mindful of your expenses.

- **Try Your Luck**: A casino within the hotel invites you to test your fortunes at the slots or tables.

- **Concierge Assistance**: Optimize your stay by consulting the concierge for activity and excursion suggestions.

Prime Location:

Situated in the heart of Corfu Town on Garitsa Bay, the Corfu Palace offers proximity to key attractions such as the Old Town, Spianada Square, and Pontikonissi Island.

Safety Measures:

- Rest easy at the Corfu Palace, equipped with 24-hour security and a CCTV system for a secure stay.

Facilities and Comforts:

Enjoy a range of amenities, including:

- Two pools (indoor and outdoor)

- A spa

- A casino

- Multiple dining venues

- A fitness center

- A business center

- Meeting rooms

- A nightclub

Corfu City Marina Hotel

Arrival Details:

- Find our hotel at Donzelot 15, Kerkira 491 00, Greece, conveniently situated near both the Old Town and the New Fortress.

- From the airport, a taxi ride is an estimated €15-€20, or opt for the nearby bus stop for island-wide connectivity.

Operating Information:

- Our reception is at your service 24/7 for seamless check-ins and assistance.

- Savor delectable meals at our restaurant during breakfast, lunch, and dinner, while the bar welcomes you until late.

Dining Costs:

- Enjoy complimentary breakfast with your stay.

- For lunch and dinner, prices range from €10-€20 per person. Alternatively, explore nearby eateries for budget-friendly options.

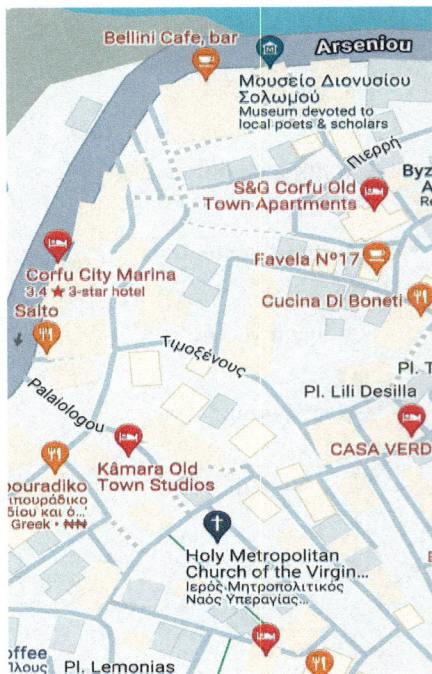

Local Insights:

- Upgrade your experience with a sea-view room for breathtaking vistas.

- •Seek local recommendations from our reception for the best Corfu Town activities.

- Stroll along the picturesque Esplanade, offering captivating sea views.

- Delight in Corfiot cuisine like pastitsada or sofrito, available both in-house and at nearby establishments.

Exploration Tips:

- Immerse yourself in the heart of Corfu Town, a hub for attractions like the Old Town, New Fortress, and the Esplanade.

- Explore charming streets, filled with shops, restaurants, and bars in the vicinity.

Security Assurance:

- Rest easy in our secure location with 24/7 security and in-room safes for your valuables.

Amenities Overview:

- Our hotel boasts a restaurant, bar, lounge, and beach access for your enjoyment.

- Relax by the swimming pool, sun terrace, or stay fit in our fitness center.

- Stay connected with complimentary Wi-Fi during your stay.

Boutique Stays

Explore the heart of Corfu and discover a realm of distinctive charm that goes beyond mere accommodation. Boutique stays in this vibrant destination offer more than just a place to rest; they provide immersive experiences resonating with intimacy, luxury, and personalized touches, inviting you to delve into the essence of Corfu's beauty and culture.

What Makes Boutique Stays Unique?

Boutique accommodations stand out with their commitment to individuality, reflecting local culture and history. Unlike larger hotels, these stays offer a unique character evident in their architecture, decor, and personalized service. Each boutique stay is a story, unfolding through an ambiance crafted for comfort and a genuine sense of place.

Discover Exceptional Boutique Stays:

Siora Vittoria Boutique Hotel - In the Heart of Corfu Town: Experience the spirit of Corfu's rich history at Siora Vittoria Boutique Hotel. Housed in a meticulously restored neoclassical building, this gem seamlessly blends period charm with modern luxury. The intimate atmosphere, personalized concierge service, and tasteful decor make Siora Vittoria a haven for those seeking heritage and contemporary allure.

37

Corfu Palace - Where Elegance Meets Serenity:

Perched near the historic Old Town, Corfu Palace epitomizes luxury and tranquility. Surrounded by lush gardens and overlooking the Ionian Sea, this boutique stay offers opulent rooms and attentive staff, creating an immersion into a world where elegance meets serenity.

Advantages of Boutique Stays:

Personalized Service:

- Boutique stays excel in providing personalized service, catering to individual needs with customized recommendations and attentive concierge services.

Attention to Detail:

- Every element in boutique stays contributes to a unique and memorable ambiance, with handpicked furnishings and curated decor elevating the experience.

Intimate Atmosphere:

- The smaller scale fosters a sense of community and exclusivity, creating a space where warmth and allure converge beyond the typical hotel experience.

Immersive Experiences:

- Beyond accommodation, boutique stays offer curated experiences connecting guests with local culture. From guided tours to exclusive access to events, these stays allow guests to truly immerse themselves in the destination.

Choosing a boutique stay in Corfu means embracing a narrative woven with elegance, culture, and personalized care. These establishments are portals to the heart of Corfu, inviting you to embark on a journey that captures the essence of this enchanting island.

Next, let's uncover budget-friendly options that promise an enriching experience without compromising quality.

Budget-Friendly Options

Exploring the Charms of Affordable Corfu:

Corfu beckons, and you don't need a hefty budget to revel in its enchanting beauty. The island extends a welcoming embrace to budget-conscious travelers, offering a diverse range of economical choices. Let's unravel the significance of these options and share some wallet-friendly suggestions for an economical and memorable Corfu experience.

The Significance of Budget-Friendly Choices:

Corfu's allure spans across different traveler profiles, emphasizing the need for accessible options. These choices not only cater to varying budgets but also contribute to a more inclusive travel experience, ensuring that the island remains a captivating destination for adventurers and savvy explorers alike.

Economical Gems for Discerning Travelers:

- Zefiros Traditional Hotel
- Affordable Charm in Corfu Town

Nestled in the heart of Corfu Town, Zefiros Traditional Hotel seamlessly combines charm with affordability. This family-run establishment offers cozy rooms adorned with traditional elements, creating a warm and inviting ambiance. Its central location allows easy exploration of Corfu's historical landmarks on foot, making it an ideal choice for comfort-conscious travelers.

- Anna Pension
- Tranquil Seaside Retreat on a Budget

For those seeking a peaceful coastal escape without breaking the bank, Anna Pension in Agios Gordios is the perfect find. A short stroll from the beach, this family-friendly guesthouse provides simple yet comfortable rooms. The village surroundings offer an authentic glimpse into local life, and proximity to the beach ensures constant access to sun, sea, and relaxation.

- Arcadion Hotel
- Elegant Affordability in Corfu Town

Discover the budget-friendly elegance of Arcadion Hotel, situated in the heart of Corfu Town. This hidden gem seamlessly blends style and affordability, with tastefully designed rooms offering a contemporary charm. Enjoy a comfortable retreat amidst the city's vibrant energy, immersing yourself in the cultural tapestry of Corfu Town without breaking the bank.

Practical Pointers for Budget Travelers:

Flexible Travel Dates: Opt for shoulder seasons to capitalize on budget-friendly accommodation and flight prices. Flexibility in travel dates opens avenues for lower rates and a more serene experience.

Accommodation Booking Platforms: Leverage online platforms for accommodation deals that align with your budget and preferences. These platforms provide a variety of options, ensuring a tailored and economical stay.

Local Eateries Exploration: Immerse yourself in Corfu's culinary delights by dining at affordable, family-run establishments. Enjoy the island's traditional cuisine without straining your budget, savoring a palette of delicious flavors.

Embrace Public Transportation: Choose cost-effective public transportation to explore beyond tourist hubs. Buses and local ferries provide affordable means to uncover hidden gems and experience the authentic charm of Corfu.

Free and Low-Cost Activities: Corfu boasts an array of free and low-cost activities. Explore quaint villages, embark on scenic hikes, or unwind on public beaches, allowing you to embrace the island's beauty without significant expenses.

Negotiation Skills: When engaging in local markets or services, don't shy away from negotiating prices. Depending on circumstances, vendors may be amenable to offering discounts, adding an extra layer of savings to your journey.

Corfu's budget-friendly options not only meet practical needs but also enhance your exploration by fostering a deeper connection with local culture. Embrace affordability for an authentic and inclusive adventure on this captivating island. Now, let's navigate the distinct districts of Corfu, each boasting its own allure and attractions for the discerning traveler.

Map Of Corfu

Potamos
Ποταμός

fra
ρρά

24

MANTOUKI
MANTOYKI

Corfu
Κέρκυρα

Alepou
Αλεπού

Corfu
International
Airport
"Ioannis..."

Ag. Vlasios
Αγ. Βλάσιος

Kanali
Κανάλι

Kompitsi
Κομπίτσι

Mon Repos
Μον Ρεπό

ΨΗΣΤΑΡΙΑ
ΓΙΑΝΝΙΤΣΗΣ
ΓΙΑΝΝΙΤΣΗΣ

Kastania
Καστανιά

Μονή Παναγίας
Βλαχερνών

Viros
Βίρος

Perama
Πέραμα

tiones
ιτιώνες

25

Souleika
Σουλαϊκα

des
ὸες

Monestary
Agias Paraskeuis
Ιερά Μονή Αγίας
Παρασκευής

The Achilleion Palace
Αχίλλειο

Agii Deka
Άγιοι Δέκα

25

Angsana Corfu

s

Ano Garouna
Άνω Γαρούνα

Benitses
Μπενίτσες

Kato Garouna
Κάτω Γαρούνα

Makrata
Μακράτα

Dafnata
Δαφνάτα

Taverna
arily closed

Pavliana
Παυλιανα

TSAKI
ΤΣΑΚΙ

Kornata

Map Of Paleokastritsa

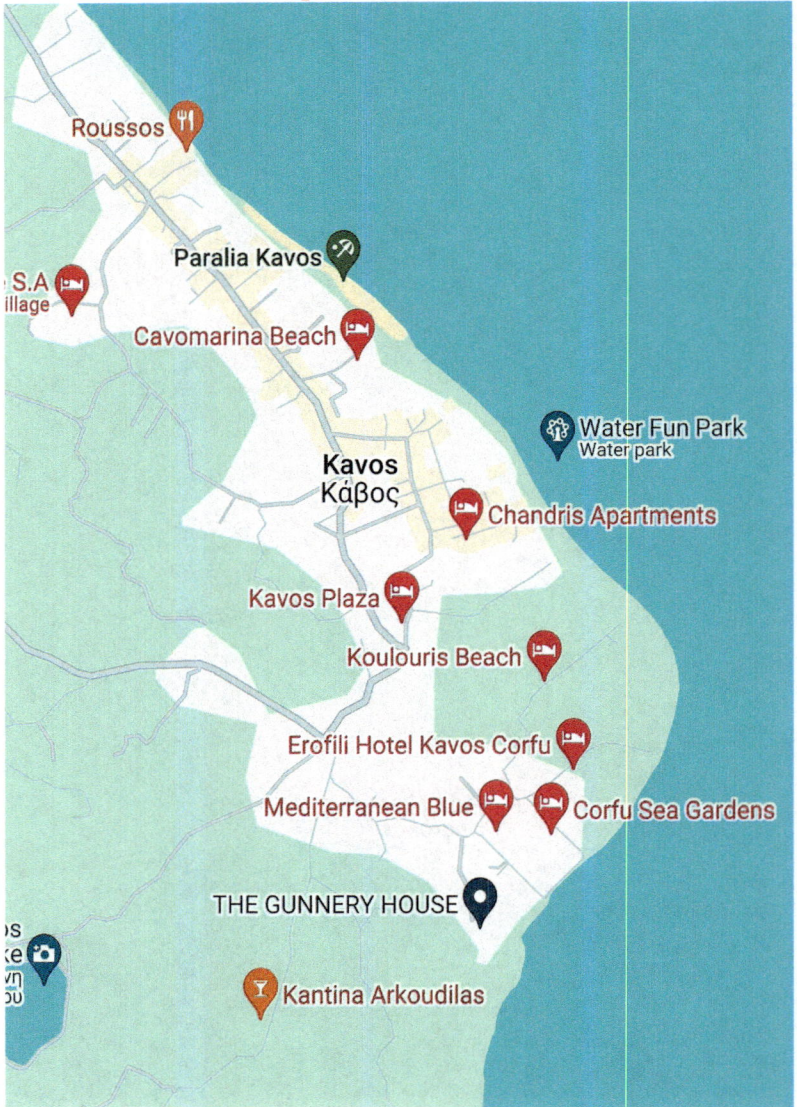

Map Of Kavos

Roussos

Paralia Kavos

S.A
illage

Cavomarina Beach

Water Fun Park
Water park

Kavos
Κάβος

Chandris Apartments

Kavos Plaza

Koulouris Beach

Erofili Hotel Kavos Corfu

Mediterranean Blue

Corfu Sea Gardens

THE GUNNERY HOUSE

os
ke
νη
ου

Kantina Arkoudilas

Map Of Kanoni

Green Buses
Terminal - KTEL
ΚΤΕΛ Κέρκυρας

Leof. Dim

Garitsa Grove
Άλσος Γαρίτσας

Alkinoou

Flexy Luggage

25

Avli Restaurant Corfu
Αυλή

Alkiviadou Dari

Windmill

Mon Repos Beach
Παραλία Μον Ρεπό

Dairpfela

Corfu
International
Airport
"Ioannis..."

Feakon

Artis

Museum of Palaiopolis
- Mon Repos
Μουσείο Παλαιόπολης
- Mon Repos

Mon Repos
Μον Ρεπό

Narsikas

Analipsi

Mon Repos Beach
Dock Kardaki
Προβλήτα Παραλίας
Μον Ρεπό Κάρδάκι

Ancient Greek Doric
Temple of Kardaki

Diellas Supermarket
ΣΟΥΠΕΡ ΜΑΡΚΕΤ
DIELLAS

Divani Corfu Palace

Narsikas

ό Κανονιού
Soccer field

Μονή Παναγίας
Κασσωπίτρας

CORFU TOURIST
SERVICES, Corfu...

Ariti Grand Hotel Corfu

Villa Sylva

Cafe Kanoni
Καφέ Κανόνι

46

City Guides

Corfu Town

Situated along the eastern coast of the island, Corfu Town, also known as Kerkyra, is a captivating fusion of Venetian, French, and British influences. This charming destination effortlessly withstands the passage of time, offering a journey through history, culture, and vibrant city life. Join us on a virtual expedition through the enchanting Corfu Town, uncovering its iconic landmarks, local markets, and the distinctive atmosphere that makes it a gem in the Ionian Sea.

Landmarks and Architectural Marvels

Liston Promenade: The pulsating heart of Corfu Town resides on the Liston Promenade. Reflecting the elegance of Paris' Rue de Rivoli, this sophisticated esplanade features arched colonnades, providing a timeless setting. Meander along the promenade, savor a coffee at a traditional café, and immerse yourself in the lively ambiance.

Spianada Square: Enveloped by remarkable buildings and historic landmarks, Spianada Square stands as one of Europe's largest squares. The Maitland Monument, a tribute to British rule, and the lush Spianada Gardens offer a peaceful escape within urban sophistication.

Old and New Fortresses: Dominating the skyline, the Old and New Fortresses serve as custodians of Corfu Town. Explore the intricate passages and battlements of the Old Fortress for panoramic views, while the New Fortress provides insight into the island's strategic history.

Saint Spyridon Church: The sky-piercing bell tower of Saint Spyridon Church beckons visitors to delve into its rich history and Byzantine architecture. Inside, the relics of Saint Spyridon attract pilgrims and history enthusiasts alike.

Corfu Archaeological Museum: Uncover the island's history at the Corfu Archaeological Museum. From ancient artifacts to medieval sculptures, the museum presents a captivating journey through Corfu's archaeological treasures.

Local Shops and Authentic Experiences

Corfu Old Town Market: Immerse yourself in the vibrant Corfu Old Town Market, where local vendors offer a diverse array of products. From fresh produce and spices to handmade crafts, this market captures the essence of daily life.

KANTOUNIA: Stroll through the narrow lanes of KANTOUNIA, the historic Jewish Quarter, where antique shops, boutiques, and artisanal stores entice. Discover unique souvenirs, handmade jewelry, and vintage finds in this charming district.

Cafés and Tavernas: Adorned with charming cafés and traditional tavernas, Corfu Town invites you to savor a leisurely meal in a courtyard shaded by bougainvillea or enjoy a frappé in a café overlooking Spianada Square. Each establishment radiates its own charm and authenticity.

The Unique Atmosphere

Corfu Town isn't just a destination; it's an immersive experience. The seamless blend of architectural grandeur, local flavors, and a lively atmosphere creates a canvas where every street corner narrates a story. The melodies of street musicians fill the air, and the vibrant colors of laundry hanging from balconies add an everyday authenticity to the historic backdrop.

As you traverse Corfu Town, let its unique atmosphere be your guide. Lose yourself in its narrow alleys, uncover hidden gems, and savor the blend of past and present that defines this enchanting town. Next, join us on a journey to Paleokastritsa, a coastal paradise that captivates with its natural beauty and spiritual significance.

Paleokastritsa

As you journey
northwest from Corfu
Town, a coastal gem
named Paleokastritsa
unfolds its beauty along
winding roads. Set
between olive-clad hills
and the crystalline
Ionian Sea,
Paleokastritsa
captivates with its
stunning landscapes
and spiritual charm.
Let's delve into the
captivating panorama of
Paleokastritsa,
uncovering its scenic
wonders and distinctive
features that make it a
compelling destination.

Coastal Marvels

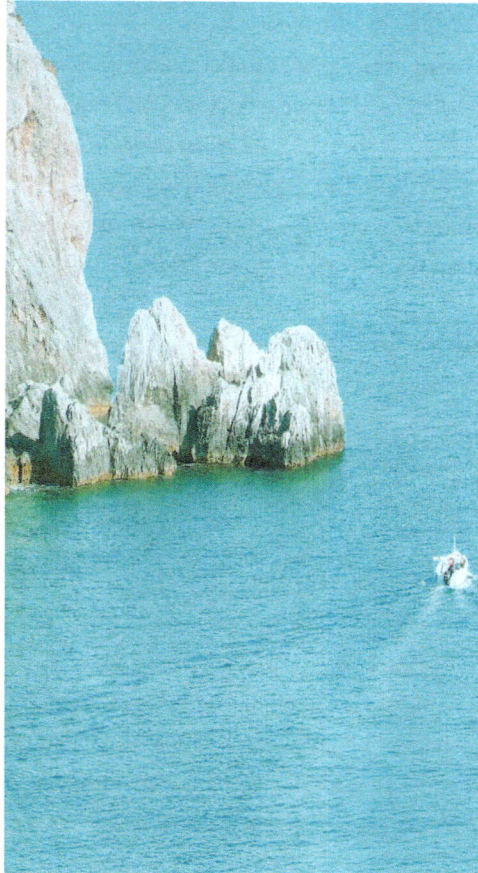

Turquoise Waters and Secluded Coves: Paleokastritsa is famed for its enchanting turquoise waters hugging the rugged coastline. Discover hidden coves and private beaches where the Ionian Sea reveals its pristine allure. The contrast of emerald-green hills against the azure sea creates a visual harmony resonating with tranquility.

Paleokastritsa Monastery: Perched on a hill with a sea view, the Paleokastritsa Monastery stands as both a spiritual haven and an observatory for panoramic vistas. Dating back to the 13th century, the monastery invites exploration of its Byzantine architecture adorned with vibrant frescoes. The serene surroundings add a touch of divine tranquility to the coastal landscape.

Boat Excursions and Coastal Caves: Embark on boat trips along Paleokastritsa's coast to uncover hidden sea caves and quiet beaches. These tours offer an intimate exploration of the area's geological wonders, allowing you to witness the play of light and shadow on the rugged cliffs.

Exploration Highlights

Angelokastro: For the adventurous, a trip to the nearby Angelokastro is essential. This ancient fortress, perched on Corfu's highest peak, not only offers historical intrigue but also provides breathtaking views of the surrounding landscapes. The trek to Angelokastro is a scenic adventure rewarding explorers with a sense of accomplishment and awe-inspiring vistas.

Theotokos Monastery: Tucked in the hills above Paleokastritsa, Theotokos Monastery offers a serene escape from coastal bustle. Surrounded by lush greenery, the monastery provides a peaceful retreat for reflection and panoramic views of the Ionian Sea.

Paleokastritsa Beach: The main beach is a haven of relaxation, where sun-seekers can unwind on pebbled shores and take refreshing dips in clear waters. Bordering the beach are traditional tavernas offering local delicacies, creating a perfect blend of seaside indulgence and culinary delights.

What Sets Paleokastritsa Apart

Spiritual Atmosphere: Paleokastritsa exudes a spiritual atmosphere with its monasteries and hillside retreats creating an ambiance of tranquility. Whether exploring the historic Paleokastritsa Monastery or seeking solitude at Theotokos Monastery, the area invites moments of contemplation and connection with nature.

Scenic Variety: The diverse landscapes, from rugged cliffs and hidden sea caves to serene beaches and lush hills, showcase Paleokastritsa's natural beauty. The area offers a rich tapestry of scenery that captivates the senses.

Genuine Greek Hospitality: Local tavernas and family-run establishments embody the warmth of Greek hospitality. Visitors can savor traditional Corfiot dishes, freshly caught seafood, and regional wines while enjoying the genuine friendliness of the locals.

Paleokastritsa, with its coastal splendor and spiritual ambiance, beckons travelers to explore a realm where nature, history, and authenticity intertwine. Whether seeking adventurous hikes, serene moments of reflection, or the pleasure of sun and sea, Paleokastritsa awaits as a timeless sanctuary along Corfu's picturesque shores. Next, let's journey to the vibrant coastal haven of Kavos, where lively energy and endless entertainment converge.

Kavos

As you journey to the southern tip of Corfu, the serene landscapes give way to the lively coastal haven of Kavos. Known for its vibrant ambiance and non-stop entertainment, Kavos beckons travelers seeking a perfect fusion of sun-soaked beaches and pulsating nightlife. Let's delve into the dynamic energy of Kavos, exploring its lively nightlife, inviting beaches, and unique attractions that define this bustling coastal gem.

Nightlife Extravaganza

Beachfront Social Hubs: Kavos is renowned for its vibrant nightlife, and the beachfront is where the party comes to life. Beach bars and clubs line the shores, providing a dynamic mix of music, dance, and seaside revelry. From sunset cocktails to all-night dance sessions, Kavos ensures that the night is as exhilarating as the day.

Late-Night Hotspots: The heart of Kavos pulsates with energy after dark. Immerse yourself in the vibrant atmosphere of late-night venues hosting international DJs, themed parties, and live performances. Kavos transforms into a nocturnal playground where the music is contagious, and the celebration is boundless.

Sun-Soaked Beaches

Golden Sands of Kavos Beach: Kavos Beach, with its golden sands and crystal-clear waters, is a playground by day and a lively hub as the sun sets. Relax on sunbeds, try water sports, or simply bask in the Mediterranean sun. The beach offers a range of activities, from jet-skiing to beach volleyball.

Island Discovery: Kavos serves as a gateway to nearby islands and hidden coves. Embark on island-hopping adventures, where boat trips take you to secluded beaches, crystal-clear lagoons, and snorkeling havens. The coastal beauty around Kavos extends beyond the mainland to the hidden gems scattered across the Ionian Sea.

Distinctive Attractions

Cape Asprokavos: Cape Asprokavos, the southernmost point of Corfu, is a rugged headland offering panoramic views of the sea and surrounding landscapes. The cliffs provide an ideal vantage point for breathtaking sunsets, creating a serene contrast to the lively energy of Kavos.

Aqua Park Adventure: For a break from the beach, Aqua Park Kavos offers a day of family-friendly fun. The water park features thrilling slides, lazy rivers, and splash pools, providing a refreshing and entertaining escape from the sun-soaked activities of the coast.

The Pulse of Kavos

Kavos pulses with infectious energy. Whether you're embracing the vibrant nightlife, sunbathing on inviting beaches, or exploring unique attractions, Kavos ensures every moment is an adventure. The juxtaposition of lively entertainment and natural beauty creates a unique atmosphere captivating the hearts of visitors.

Practical Tips for Enjoying Kavos

Nightlife Planning: With its renowned nightlife, plan your evenings to experience the diverse array of beach parties, club events, and live performances. The nightlife scene in Kavos is dynamic, catering to every taste.

Explore Beyond the Main Hub: While the main strip is bustling, take time to explore the surrounding areas. Hidden beaches, seaside tavernas, and quieter spots await those who venture beyond the bustling center.

Water Sports Thrills: Kavos Beach is not just for sunbathing; it's a playground for water sports enthusiasts. Try jet-skiing, parasailing, or banana boat rides for an adrenaline-pumping experience.

Kavos invites you to surrender to its vibrant rhythm, where the days are sun-soaked, and the nights are alive with music and celebration. Whether you're a party enthusiast, a sun worshiper, or an adventurer,

Kavos promises an exhilarating escape along the southern shores of Corfu.

Kanoni

On the eastern coast of Corfu lies the captivating district of Kanoni, a harmonious blend of natural splendor and historical intrigue. Perched on a hill with a commanding view of the Ionian Sea, Kanoni beckons explorers to uncover its charm through stunning landscapes and a rich historical tapestry. Join us on a journey to Kanoni as we unravel its allure, exploring viewpoints, historical sites, and engaging activities for an enriching experience.

Panoramic Vistas

Vlacherna Monastery: Gazing at Kanoni, the eye-catching Vlacherna Monastery stands proudly on a narrow causeway, overlooking the sea like a sentinel. Offering a picturesque panorama, this vantage point reveals the Kanoni peninsula, Corfu's airport runway, and the distant Mouse Island (Pontikonisi).

Mouse Island (Pontikonisi): Accessible by boat, Mouse Island presents a tranquil retreat. Crowned by the Byzantine Vlacherna Monastery, the islet's lush greenery against the azure waters provides a serene backdrop. This viewpoint allows for an appreciation of the verdant landscapes and the peaceful beauty of the surrounding sea.

Historical Gems

Mon Repos Palace: A short drive away, Mon Repos Palace, a neoclassical masterpiece surrounded by lush gardens, holds historical significance as the birthplace of Prince Philip, the Duke of Edinburgh. Stroll through the estate, explore the palace's interiors, and soak in the historical ambiance.

Church of Panagia Vlacherna: Adjacent to Vlacherna Monastery, this church showcases Byzantine architecture and religious devotion. Step inside to admire intricate frescoes and icons, reflecting the deep cultural and spiritual heritage of the region.

Enriching Activities

Boat Tours and Cruises: Explore Kanoni and Mouse Island's coastline by joining a boat tour or cruise. The crystal-clear waters offer opportunities for swimming, snorkeling, and capturing the scenic coastal beauty.

Kanoni Promenade: A leisurely stroll along the Kanoni promenade offers stunning views of Vlacherna Monastery, Mouse Island, and the distant hills of Corfu. Cafés along the promenade provide a perfect setting to savor a coffee while enjoying the breathtaking scenery.

Kanoni's Unique Appeal

Serene Landscapes: Kanoni's charm lies in its serene landscapes and breathtaking views. Whether gazing over the Ionian Sea from Vlacherna Monastery or exploring the verdant islet of Pontikonisi, Kanoni captivates with its natural beauty and tranquility.

Rich History: Steeped in history, Kanoni's landmarks, including Mon Repos Palace and the Church of Panagia Vlacherna, offer glimpses into Corfu's rich past. Kanoni serves as a bridge between the island's cultural heritage and its natural wonders.

Cultural Exploration: Kanoni invites cultural exploration, from admiring Byzantine architecture to visiting the birthplace of Prince Philip. The district provides opportunities to connect with Corfu's cultural identity through its historical sites and religious landmarks.

In Kanoni, with its panoramic viewpoints, historical treasures, and cultural richness, visitors are treated to a diverse showcase of Corfu's allure. Whether seeking moments of reflection at a centuries-old monastery or immersing oneself in the historical narratives of a neoclassical palace, Kanoni promises a journey through time and beauty.

Cultural Experiences

Museums and Galleries

Corfu's cultural legacy unfolds like a vivid tapestry, interweaving threads of art, history, and artifacts. Explore the island's museums and galleries for a journey through time, uncovering stories, artistic expressions, and historical treasures that define Corfu's identity.

Corfu Archaeological Museum

Unearth Ancient Wonders:

Centrally located in Corfu Town, the Corfu Archaeological Museum is a repository of artifacts chronicling the island's rich history. From ancient sculptures and pottery to intricate jewelry and coins, the museum offers a captivating glimpse into Corfu's classical past, featuring highlights like the Gorgon pediment from the Temple of Artemis, a testament to the island's ties to Greek mythology.

Museum of Asian Art

Far East Odyssey:

Nestled in the Palace of St. Michael and St. George in Corfu Town, the Museum of Asian Art transports visitors to the exotic realms of the Far East. Its extensive collection spans centuries and cultures, showcasing Asian artifacts, paintings, and sculptures. Marvel at intricately crafted

Chinese ceramics, Japanese prints, and delicate Indian miniatures, providing a captivating cross-cultural exploration.

Byzantine Museum of Antivouniotissa

Artistic Reverence through Time:

Tucked away in a charming corner of Corfu Town, the Byzantine Museum of Antivouniotissa unveils the spiritual and artistic heritage of Byzantium. Explore a remarkable collection of religious icons, frescoes, and artifacts dating from the 15th to the 19th centuries, offering insights into the Byzantine influence on Corfu's cultural landscape.

Corfu Museum of Asian-European Art

East-West Fusion:

Situated in the historic Palace of St. Michael and St. George, the Corfu Museum of Asian-European Art is a fusion of Western and Eastern artistic expressions. The museum showcases a diverse range of European and Asian artworks, inviting visitors to explore the dynamic dialogue between two distinct cultural worlds.

Ionian Academy

Intellectual Oasis:

The Ionian Academy, in Corfu Town, stands as a testament to the island's intellectual legacy. Founded in 1824, the academy played a pivotal role in the intellectual and cultural development of the Ionian Islands. Today, it hosts cultural events and exhibitions, contributing to Corfu's ongoing narrative of enlightenment and intellectual exploration.

Cultural Enrichment in Galleries

Municipal Gallery of Corfu:

- Housed in the Palace of St. Michael and St. George, the Municipal Gallery of Corfu showcases a diverse collection of Greek paintings from the 19th and 20th centuries. Take a visual journey through the evolution of Greek art, featuring works by prominent artists.

Artistic Expression in Local Galleries:

- Beyond the prominent museums, Corfu boasts a thriving local art scene with numerous galleries. Explore the vibrant works of local artists, capturing the essence of Corfu's landscapes, traditions, and contemporary perspectives.

Cultural Diversity in Corfu's Museums and Galleries

Corfu's museums and galleries mirror the island's multifaceted identity—rooted in ancient civilizations, influenced by Byzantine traditions, and open to the cultural currents of Europe and Asia. Each institution offers a unique lens through which visitors can engage with Corfu's rich cultural heritage, whether by admiring classical sculptures, exploring Byzantine art, or appreciating the interplay of East and West.

Now, let's dive into the vibrant tapestry of Corfu's festivals and events, celebrating the island's cultural vitality throughout the year.

62

Festivals and Events

Delve into Corfu's captivating history, a blend of ancient Greek roots and influences from Venetian and British eras. Join us on a journey through the island's tapestry of festivals, immersing yourself in its lively spirit.

Easter Revelry

Witness Unique Paschal Traditions:

Corfu's Easter celebrations are globally acclaimed for their grandeur and distinctive customs. On Holy Saturday, experience the "First Resurrection," where locals toss clay pots from windows, creating a symphony of sound. At midnight, the Resurrection service unfolds in Corfu Town's streets, climaxing with the smashing of clay pots at Spianada Square. The mesmerizing glow of candles and the splendid atmosphere make Corfu's Easter an unforgettable spectacle.

Corfu Summer Festival

Cultural Extravaganza in Corfu Town:

From June to September, the Corfu Summer Festival transforms the island into a cultural haven. Historic venues like the Liston Promenade and the Old and New Fortresses host a diverse range of events, from classical music concerts to dance recitals. This festival enriches the island's cultural fabric, drawing both locals and visitors.

Corfu Beer Festival

Craft Beer and Musical Bliss:

In September, the Corfu Beer Festival beckons beer and music enthusiasts. Amidst the scenic backdrop of Corfu's New Fortress, savor local and international craft beers while enjoying live music performances. It's an immersive experience in a lush setting.

Achilleion Palace Events

Cultural Splendor Amidst Royalty:

Throughout the year, the Achilleion Palace hosts cultural events in its regal setting. From classical music concerts to art exhibitions, visitors can bask in the grandeur of the palace while enjoying cultural performances.

Local Celebrations and Feasts

Village Festivals Alive with Energy:

Corfu's villages pulsate with life during local festivals and religious feasts, known as "panigiria." These events feature traditional music, dance, and culinary delights, providing a genuine glimpse into the island's community spirit.

Travel Tips

- **Plan Around Easter for Cultural Riches**: Schedule your visit to Corfu around Easter to witness the spectacular Paschal traditions and the Resurrection service.

- **Corfu Summer Festival Schedule**: If visiting during the summer, check the schedule for the Corfu Summer Festival. Enjoy diverse cultural performances against the backdrop of historic landmarks.

- **Embrace Local Spirit at Panigiria**: Discover local panigiria in villages for an authentic experience of Corfu's cultural heritage with traditional music, dancing, and local delicacies.

- **Craft Beer Exploration**: Craft beer enthusiasts should plan around the Corfu Beer Festival in September, a perfect blend of beer tasting and live music.

Corfu's festivals embody the island's dynamic cultural tapestry, inviting travelers to engage with traditions, arts, and community celebrations. Whether captivated by the grandeur of Easter, the cultural spectacles of summer, or the lively ambiance of local festivals, Corfu awaits with open arms, welcoming you to its vibrant spirit.

Traditional Cuisine

Corfu, a culinary symphony, harmonizes Greek, Italian, and Mediterranean influences in a tapestry of rich flavors. Let your taste buds dance through the island's gastronomic heritage with these must-try dishes and local eateries.

Must-Try Dishes

Pastitsada:
Slow-cooked meat in a tomato-based sauce, pastitsada, a hearty classic, is served over pasta or mashed potatoes, infused with aromatic spices.

Sofrito:
Tender veal marinated in garlic and white wine, slow-cooked to perfection. Sofrito shines when paired with rice or mashed potatoes, showcasing its savory flavors.

Bourdeto:
A spicy fisherman's stew featuring red scorpionfish in a bold tomato and chili sauce, highlighting the island's abundant seafood.

Kumquat Liqueur:
Sip on Corfu's renowned kumquat liqueur for a refreshing taste of this unique citrus fruit.

Pastelaki:
A sweet treat capturing Corfu's essence, pastelaki combines honey, almonds, and sesame seeds in a delightful confection.

Popular Local Eateries

Taverna Agni:
In Agni Bay, Taverna Agni offers a picturesque setting to savor fresh seafood, from grilled octopus to traditional moussaka.

Rouvas Taverna:
Nestled in Corfu Town, Rouvas Taverna is a family-run spot known for authentic Corfiot cuisine, featuring pastitsada and sofrito.

Taverna Tou Psiri:
A beloved spot in Pelekas village, Taverna Tou Psiri serves a variety of Corfiot dishes with a focus on fresh, locally sourced ingredients.

Bella Ellada:
Overlooking Liston Promenade, Bella Ellada provides a sophisticated dining experience with a modern twist on traditional dishes like bourdeto.

To Perasma:
In Vatos village, To Perasma offers a charming, family-run taverna with warm hospitality and traditional Corfiot dishes.

Dining Tips

Explore Local Markets:
Corfu Town's local markets unveil fresh produce, spices, and regional specialties, providing an authentic glimpse into the island's culinary ingredients.

Try Corfiot Sweets:

Indulge in delightful local sweets like mandolato (nougat) and pasta flora (fruit preserves in shortcrust pastry).

Embrace the Meze Culture:

Enjoy the joy of sharing small dishes with meze-style menus, allowing you to savor a variety of flavors in one sitting.

Ask for Local Recommendations:

Seek recommendations from locals for hidden culinary gems and their favorite dishes when dining in Corfu.

Corfu's traditional cuisine, a celebration of flavors, narrates stories of history, culture, and natural bounty. As you relish savory classics and sweet delights, you embark on a journey through the island's culinary heritage. Next, lace up your hiking boots for an exploration of Corfu's outdoor wonders, from scenic trails to invigorating water activities.

Outdoor Adventures

Hiking Trails

Corfu unfolds its diverse landscapes, inviting avid explorers to don their hiking boots and traverse scenic trails. From coastal paths offering breathtaking sea views to inland routes weaving through lush hillsides, Corfu stands as a haven for nature enthusiasts. Let's embark on a journey through some of the island's standout hiking trails, each presenting a distinctive blend of challenge, natural wonders, and captivating vistas.

Corfu Trail:

Difficulty: Moderate to Challenging
- Highlights: Stretching the length of the island, the Corfu Trail winds through olive groves, dense forests, and coastal cliffs. It unveils panoramic views of the Ionian Sea, meandering through traditional villages, delivering a comprehensive exploration of Corfu's allure.

Paleokastritsa Trail:

Difficulty: Moderate
- Highlights: This coastal trail around Paleokastritsa takes hikers along rugged cliffs with awe-inspiring views of the turquoise sea. Featuring visits to the Paleokastritsa Monastery and opportunities for secluded beach exploration, the trail encapsulates the essence of Corfu's coastal charm.

Angelokastro Trail:

Difficulty: Moderate to Challenging
- Highlights: Leading to the ancient Angelokastro fortress, this trail treats hikers to panoramic views of the island and the Ionian Sea. Winding through cypress forests, it unveils historical sites, offering both a physical challenge and a cultural journey.

Kanoni to Benitses Coastal Trail:

Difficulty: Easy to Moderate
- Highlights: This coastal trail provides a leisurely hike along the shoreline, linking the picturesque Kanoni to the charming village of Benitses. Hikers can relish sea views, pass through olive groves, and explore the traditional fishing harbor of Benitses.

Ropa Valley Trail:

Difficulty: Easy
- Highlights: Ideal for a relaxed stroll, the Ropa Valley Trail guides hikers through the island's verdant interior. Winding through vineyards, orchards, and the scenic Ropa Valley, it offers a serene escape into Corfu's lush landscapes.

Kaiser's Throne Trail:

Difficulty: Easy to Moderate
- Highlights: Named after Emperor Wilhelm II, the Kaiser's Throne Trail presents stunning views of Corfu's south coast. Culminating

in a viewpoint resembling a throne, hikers can savor the panoramic vista and the azure waters below.

Hiking Tips:

1. Wear Sturdy Footwear: To navigate uneven terrain, don sturdy hiking boots for stability and comfort.

2. Carry Ample Water: Stay hydrated, especially in warmer months; bring enough water for refreshment along the trails.

3. Check Trail Conditions: Before setting out, assess current trail conditions, as some paths may be more challenging after heavy rainfall.

4. Respect Nature and Wildlife: Corfu's diverse flora and fauna deserve respect; avoid disturbing wildlife during your hikes.

5. Trail Maps and Guides: Consider using trail maps or guides, particularly for longer or more challenging routes. Local tourist offices may provide helpful resources.

Corfu's hiking trails promise an enchanting blend of natural beauty, historical charm, and diverse difficulty levels. Whether seeking mountain-summit panoramas or coastal walks along turquoise waters, the island's trails promise a memorable outdoor adventure. Next, let's plunge into the inviting waters surrounding Corfu and explore the plethora of water activities awaiting adventure seekers.

Water Activities

Corfu's stunning coastline is a haven for water enthusiasts, combining serenity and thrills. Delve into the refreshing embrace of the Ionian waters with a variety of aquatic adventures.

Paleokastritsa Snorkeling:

- Explore the crystal-clear waters and underwater wonders of Paleokastritsa. This coastal gem offers secluded coves and sea caves, providing an ideal setting for snorkelers to witness vibrant marine life.

Paxos and Antipaxos Boat Tours:

- Embark on a boat tour to the neighboring islands of Paxos and Antipaxos. Cruise through the Ionian Sea, discovering hidden caves and pristine beaches. These day excursions also offer swimming stops and a taste of local cuisine.

Windsurfing in Agios Georgios:

- Experience the thrill of windsurfing on the wide sandy beach of Agios Georgios. Glide over the waves, feeling the rush of the wind. Rentals and lessons are available for both beginners and experienced windsurfers.

Kayaking along Corfu's Coastline:

- Paddle along Corfu's scenic coastline with guided kayak tours. Explore hidden coves and rugged cliffs while enjoying the tranquility of the Ionian Sea. Both leisurely paddles and more adventurous routes are available.

Parasailing in Ipsos:

- Feel the adrenaline in Ipsos with parasailing adventures. Soar into the sky, towed by a speedboat, and enjoy breathtaking aerial views of the coastline and surroundings.

Scuba Diving in Kassiopi:

- Dive into the underwater wonders around Kassiopi. Discover rich marine life, underwater caves, and captivating dive sites suitable for all levels of divers.

Jet Skiing in Gouvia:

- Seek an adrenaline rush with jet skiing adventures in Gouvia. Ride the waves, exploring the coastline for a thrilling water experience.

Water Activity Tips:

Safety First:

- Prioritize safety by wearing appropriate gear and following guidelines for each water activity. Ensure operators adhere to safety standards for water sports.

Explore Hidden Coves:

- Take advantage of boat tours and kayaking to uncover secluded coves and hidden beaches inaccessible by land.

Snorkeling Tours:

- Join guided snorkeling tours with experienced instructors to explore vibrant reefs and marine life.

73

Capture the Moments:

- Bring a waterproof camera to capture the stunning underwater landscapes and your water adventures.

Respect Marine Life:

- Maintain a respectful distance from marine life during snorkeling or scuba diving. Preserve the natural beauty of the underwater environment.

Corfu's aquatic activities promise a dynamic blend of exploration and relaxation. Glide over waves, explore hidden caves, and discover the underwater wonders, each unveiling a unique facet of Corfu's allure. Next, let's meander through the island's charming villages, each with its distinctive character and cultural charm.

Exploring Villages

Corfu's essence extends beyond its lively towns and dynamic coastlines, encompassing the heartwarming charm found in its idyllic villages scattered across the island. These villages narrate tales of tradition, history, and a welcoming community spirit that embraces visitors warmly. Let's venture away from the usual paths and discover some of Corfu's captivating villages, each offering a unique blend of cultural allure.

Pelekas:

Distinctive Encounters: Positioned atop a hill, Pelekas treats visitors to sweeping vistas of Corfu's west coast and the Ionian Sea. Recognized as the "Sunset Village," Pelekas earns its fame from the breathtaking sunsets witnessed at Kaiser's Throne. Immerse yourself in the bohemian ambiance, relish local delicacies at tavernas, and explore the nearby sandy haven of Kontogialos.

Lakones:

Distinctive Encounters: Nestled on the northwest coast, Lakones unveils stunning views of Paleokastritsa Bay. Meander through narrow pathways, visit traditional cafes with panoramic terraces, and indulge in local hospitality. A visit to the Bella Vista viewpoint is essential for capturing the picturesque beauty of Corfu's coastline.

Kynopiastes:

Distinctive Encounters: Brimming with traditional charm in its well-preserved architecture and village squares, Kynopiastes is renowned for its olive oil production. Delight in local delicacies at tavernas, including the famed "Bourekia" pastries. Experience the warm hospitality during local festivals.

Agios Mattheos:

Distinctive Encounters: Situated in the island's south, Agios Mattheos is surrounded by lush landscapes and traditional olive groves.

75

Uncover the village's history at the Folklore Museum, explore the 12th-century Church of Agios Mattheos, and partake in local festivals celebrating cultural traditions.

Ano Garouna:

Distinctive Encounters: Hidden in the mountains, Ano Garouna offers a serene retreat into Corfu's rural charm. Stroll through stone-paved streets, engage with amicable locals, and witness traditional agricultural practices. The village provides a tranquil atmosphere away from tourist crowds.

Chlomos:

Distinctive Encounters: A concealed gem perched on a hill overlooking the southeast coast, Chlomos boasts narrow alleys and well-preserved Venetian architecture. Revel in panoramic views and relish the timeless charm that transports visitors to a bygone era.

Tips for Exploring Villages:

Local Festivals: Discover local festivals or "panigiria" for an authentic experience of Corfu's cultural traditions, featuring traditional music, dance, and culinary delights.

Explore on Foot: Embrace the village charm on foot. Wander through cobblestone streets, interact with locals, and uncover hidden corners inaccessible by car.

Capture the Architecture: Villages like Chlomos and Lakones showcase well-preserved Venetian architecture. Capture the beauty of traditional buildings, churches, and village squares.

Taste Local Cuisine: Indulge in the culinary offerings of each village. Visit local tavernas to savor regional dishes, homemade wines, and desserts showcasing the flavors of Corfu.

Meet the Locals: Engage in conversations with locals to gain insights into their way of life, traditions, and generational stories, enriching your understanding of the village's cultural fabric.

Corfu's villages promise a serene escape, beckoning travelers to uncover the island's cultural tapestry beyond its popular attractions. Whether captivated by the panoramic views of Lakones, the traditional allure of Kynopiastes, or the bohemian spirit of Pelekas, each village extends a distinct character and a heartfelt welcome.

Now, let's navigate the practical aspects of transportation, ensuring a seamless and delightful exploration of Corfu.

Transportation

Getting Around Corfu

Discovering Corfu's captivating landscapes and diverse attractions is an adventure best undertaken with a savvy approach to transportation. Unraveling the island's secrets, from quaint villages to historic towns and serene coastlines, becomes seamless and enjoyable with a keen understanding of your travel options.

1. Car Rentals:

Benefits:

- **Flexibility**: Explore Corfu at your own pace, reaching remote destinations and hidden gems.
- **Scenic Drives**: Embark on picturesque journeys along coastal roads and through olive groves, revealing the island's natural beauty.

Tips:

- **Book in Advance**: Ensure a hassle-free experience by booking your rental car ahead, especially during peak tourist seasons.
- **Driving Conditions**: Familiarize yourself with local driving regulations, exercising caution on winding mountain roads.

2. Taxis:

Advantages:

- **Convenience**: Taxis offer a door-to-door transportation option, particularly suitable for shorter distances.
- **Local Insight**: Benefit from valuable local insights and recommendations provided by taxi drivers.

Tips:

- **Agree on Fare**: Establish the fare with the taxi driver before your journey or ensure the use of the meter.
- **Taxi Ranks**: Access designated taxi ranks in towns and popular tourist areas for convenient service.

3. Public Buses:

Benefits:

- **Cost-Effective**: Public buses provide a budget-friendly means of connecting major towns and villages.
- **Local Experience**: Immerse yourself in local life and connect with fellow travelers during bus journeys.

Tips:

- **Bus Schedule**: Check the schedule in advance, as services may vary based on the season.
- **Exact Change**: Have the exact fare ready, as drivers may not always provide change.

4. Scooter/Motorbike Rental:

Advantages:

- **Maneuverability**: Ideal for navigating narrow village streets and accessing hidden corners.
- **Parking**: Finding parking is generally easier with scooters or motorbikes.

Tips:

- **License Requirements**: Ensure you possess the appropriate license for renting scooters or motorbikes.
- **Safety Gear**: Prioritize safety by using helmets and protective gear.

5. Bicycle Rental:

Benefits:

- **Eco-Friendly**: Explore Corfu's landscapes in an environmentally conscious way with bicycle rentals.
- **Exercise**: Combine exploration with physical activity through cycling.

Tips:

- **Terrain Consideration**: Be mindful of the terrain, especially in hilly areas.
- **Safety Measures**: Follow safety guidelines and utilize bike lanes where available.

Advantages:

- **Immersive Experience**: Absorb the details of your surroundings with a more intimate walking experience.
- **Historic Towns**: Explore historic towns like Corfu Town on foot to appreciate their charm.

Tips:

- **Comfortable Footwear**: Opt for comfortable shoes, especially when exploring villages with cobblestone streets.
- **Navigation**: Utilize walking paths and explore pedestrian-friendly areas.

Corfu's diverse transportation options cater to various preferences, each unlocking a unique facet of the island's enchanting allure. Whether you opt for a scenic drive, a leisurely stroll, or any other mode, your exploration promises to be both enriching and unforgettable.

Renting a Car

Exploring Corfu by car unlocks a realm of possibilities, letting you navigate the island's varied landscapes at your own pace. This guide walks you through the ins and outs of renting a car in Corfu, outlining the advantages, potential challenges, and suggesting captivating routes to enrich your journey.

Advantages of Renting a Car:

Flexibility:

- **Discover Hidden Spots**: Venture to remote villages, secluded beaches, and less-traveled attractions, inaccessible by public transport.

Convenience:

- **Door-to-Door Freedom**: Enjoy the ease of door-to-door travel, tailoring your itinerary to suit your preferences.

Scenic Drives:

- **Coastal Marvels**: Corfu offers mesmerizing coastal roads, providing stunning views of the Ionian Sea. Enjoy the island's natural beauty through scenic drives.

Time Efficiency:

- **Optimize Your Schedule**: Save time by avoiding rigid bus or taxi schedules, creating a personalized itinerary based on your interests.

Potential Challenges:

Winding Roads:

- **Mountainous Terrain**: Some routes feature winding mountain roads with spectacular views, suitable for drivers comfortable with hilly terrains.

Parking in Towns:

- **Limited Space**: In popular towns like Corfu Town, parking may be restricted. Utilize designated areas or explore on foot in these locales.

Traffic during Peak Seasons:

- **Tourist Rush**: High tourist seasons can bring increased traffic in specific areas. Plan and travel during off-peak hours to navigate congestion.

Scenic Routes to Explore:

Paleokastritsa to Angelokastro:

- **Highlights**: Travel along the picturesque west coast, passing Paleokastritsa's clear waters to reach the ancient Angelokastro fortress.

Corfu Town to Pelekas:

- **Highlights**: Wind your way from Corfu Town to Pelekas for stunning sunsets, experiencing a blend of coastal and inland landscapes.

Kanoni to Benitses Coastal Drive:

Highlights: Revel in the east coast's beauty with a drive from Kanoni to Benitses. Enjoy sea views, traditional villages, and Benitses' charming harbor.

Agios Mattheos to Chlomos:

- **Highlights**: Journey into the island's heart, driving from Agios Mattheos to Chlomos, surrounded by olive groves and the tranquility of traditional villages.

Practical Tips for Renting a Car:

Booking in Advance:

- **Early Reservations**: Secure your rental car ahead, especially during peak seasons, for availability and competitive rates.

Driving License Requirements:

- **International Driving Permit**: If needed, ensure you have an International Driving Permit; most agencies accept your valid home country license.

Insurance Coverage:

- **Verify Coverage**: Check the rental company's insurance, considering additional coverage for off-road or mountainous driving.

Inspect the Car:

Thorough Check: Before acceptance, thoroughly inspect the car for damage, ensuring the rental agency documents any issues.
Fuel Policy:

- **Understand Policies**: Clarify the fuel policy with the agency; some operate on a full-to-full basis, requiring a full tank upon return.

Renting a car in Corfu transforms your journey, granting the liberty to explore the island's diverse regions on your terms. With the open road ahead, Corfu's scenic wonders await your discovery.

Public Transportation

Corfu boasts a practical network of public transportation options that efficiently link major towns, villages, and tourist attractions, presenting a cost-effective means for visitors to explore the island's charm. Although not as expansive as metropolitan systems, Corfu's public transit caters well to travelers seeking an authentic local experience amid picturesque landscapes. Let's delve into the available options for public transportation, ensuring a seamless island exploration.

1. Public Buses:

Network: Corfu's public bus system connects major towns, villages, and tourist hotspots. The primary station in Corfu Town facilitates routes to various island destinations.

Schedules: Bus schedules may fluctuate seasonally, with increased services during peak tourist periods. It's advisable for visitors to check schedules in advance, particularly for routes to more remote areas.

2. Bus Routes and Destinations:

Town Connections: Buses link Corfu Town with suburbs and nearby towns like Kanoni and Ipsos.

Village Routes: Several routes traverse the island's interior, reaching charming villages like Pelekas and Paleokastritsa.

Beach Access: Buses conveniently transport beachgoers to popular seaside destinations.

3. Tickets and Payment:

Ticket Purchase: Passengers can purchase tickets directly from the bus driver before boarding, with exact change recommended.

Ticket Prices: Fares are reasonable, making public buses a cost-effective mode of transportation.

4. Taxis:

Availability: Taxis are easily found in Corfu Town, major tourist areas, and at designated ranks.

Convenience: Taxis provide door-to-door service, offering a convenient option for personalized transportation.

5. Walking:

Pedestrian-Friendly Areas: Many Corfu towns and tourist spots are pedestrian-friendly, encouraging exploration on foot.

Historic Districts: Historic districts, like Corfu Town's Old Town, are best experienced on foot to fully appreciate the architecture and ambiance.

Navigating Public Transportation:

Bus Schedule Awareness:

Check schedules in advance, using tourist information centers or online resources for updated information.
Central Bus Station:

Corfu Town's central bus station serves as a hub for various routes, providing easy access to different parts of the island.

Taxi Ranks:

Designated taxi ranks in busy areas ensure convenient access to taxis.

Local Advice:

Locals are valuable sources of information regarding bus routes, schedules, and the most efficient ways to reach specific destinations. Ease of Navigation:

Corfu's public transportation serves as a practical choice for visitors looking to explore the island sans a car. While not covering every remote corner, the bus network connects to numerous popular destinations, offering a chance to embrace local life and scenic routes. Enhance your exploration by planning around bus routes, checking schedules, and seeking local insights for a comprehensive and enriching experience. Next, let's delve into practical information regarding currency, language, and health and safety for a smooth and enjoyable stay on the island.

Practical Information

Currency and Money Matters

Prepare for a seamless financial experience during your visit to Corfu by mastering the essentials of local currency, banking, and money matters. Let's delve into the practicalities, ensuring you're well-equipped to manage your finances effortlessly.

Local Currency:

Currency: Euro (€) reigns supreme in Corfu and throughout Greece. For daily transactions, keep some cash handy, as it is widely accepted. Banking Options:

- **Banks**: In Corfu Town and major towns, find banks for currency exchange and other financial needs.
- **ATMs**: Automated Teller Machines are conveniently scattered in urban areas. Stick to reputable bank-affiliated ATMs for secure cash withdrawals.

Credit Cards:

Acceptance: Visa and Mastercard are your go-to plastic companions, widely embraced in tourist spots and large establishments. For smaller venues, especially in remote areas, having some cash is advisable.

Currency Exchange Tips:

Rates: Seek competitive exchange rates at banks or authorized exchange offices.

Cash Reserves: While plastic is handy, a bit of cash comes in handy for those no-card locales.

Tipping Culture:

Gratuities: Tipping is a nice touch but not mandatory. Round up the bill or add a percentage for good service in restaurants. Tipping hotel staff and taxi drivers is customary.

Safety Considerations:

Secure Finances: Guard your valuables in crowded areas using a money belt or secure pouch.

Emergency Cash: Stash a bit of emergency cash separately for unforeseen circumstances.

Budgeting Tips:

Daily Expenses: Plan your budget for accommodation, meals, transportation, and activities.

Local Markets: Scout local markets for budget-friendly options in fresh produce, snacks, and souvenirs.

Banking Hours:

Business Days: Banks operate Monday to Friday. Schedule your banking transactions accordingly.

Currency Symbols:

Euro Symbol: Recognize the € symbol to avoid any pricing confusion. Contactless Payments:

Availability: In Corfu, contactless payments are gaining traction, especially in urban and tourist hubs. Confirm with establishments regarding their acceptance.

Corfu's financial landscape is well-tailored for visitors. Master the nuances of currency, leverage ATMs smartly, and balance cash with cards for a smooth financial journey across the island.

Language and Communication

Basic Greek Phrases:

Greetings:

- Hello - Γεια σας (Ya sas)
- Goodbye - Αντίο (An-tee-o)
- Good morning - Καλημέρα (Ka-lee-me-ra)
- Good evening - Καλησπέρα (Ka-lee-spe-ra)
- Good night - Καληνύχτα (Ka-lee-neekh-ta)

Courtesy Expressions:

- Please - Παρακαλώ (Para-ka-lo)
- Thank you - Ευχαριστώ (Ef-ha-ri-sto)
- You're welcome - Παρακαλώ (Para-ka-lo)
- Excuse me / I'm sorry - Συγγνώμη (Si-gno-mi)
- Yes - Ναι (Ne)
- No - Όχι (O-khi)

Asking for Assistance:

- Where is...? - Πού είναι...; (Pou i-ne...?)
- How much is this? - Πόσο κοστίζει αυτό; (Po-so kos-tee-zei af-to?)
- Can you help me? - Μπορείτε να με βοηθήσετε; (Bo-rei-te na me vo-i-thi-se-te?)
- I need... - Χρειάζομαι... (Khre-iaz-o-mai...)

Common Expressions:

- Excuse me, do you speak English? - Συγγνώμη, μιλάτε Αγγλικά; (Si-gno-mi, mi-la-te An-gli-ka?)
- I don't understand - Δεν καταλαβαίνω (Den ka-ta-la-ve-no)
- Where is the bathroom? - Πού είναι η τουαλέτα; (Pou i-ne ee toua-le-ta?)
- Help! - Βοήθεια! (Vo-i-thee-a!)
- Cheers! - ΥΓΕΙΑ! (Yia sou!)

Tips for Effective Communication:

Learn Basic Phrases:

- Familiarize yourself with essential Greek phrases to convey politeness and express an interest in the local language.

Speak Slowly:

- If not fluent, speak slowly and clearly for better comprehension.

Use Non-Verbal Communication:

- Employ non-verbal cues like hand gestures and facial expressions to convey meaning effectively.

Ask Locals for Pronunciation Help:

- Seek assistance from locals for proper pronunciation, demonstrating cultural respect.

Be Open to Language Exchange:

- Engage in language exchange to connect with locals and deepen cultural understanding.

Utilize Translation Apps:

- Employ translation apps for assistance with menus, signs, and written information.

Smile and Be Polite:

- A friendly demeanor and a smile contribute to positive interactions and cultural appreciation.

Learn Local Pronunciations:

- Familiarize yourself with unique Greek letter pronunciations, enhancing communication.

Connecting through language enriches travel experiences, demonstrating respect for the local culture. While English is widely understood, embracing Greek adds a personal touch to your journey, fostering meaningful connections. Next, let's focus on ensuring your health and safety during your stay in Corfu, with essential considerations and tips.

Health and Safety

Ensuring your well-being is our top priority during your stay in Corfu. Explore the island worry-free with this concise guide covering crucial health information, safety tips, and emergency contacts.

Essential Health Information:

Medical Facilities:

- Corfu boasts hospitals and clinics, including the comprehensive Corfu General Hospital in Corfu Town.

Pharmacies:

- Pharmacies are readily available in towns and tourist areas.

- Over-the-counter medications are common, but specific prescriptions may require consultation with a local doctor.

Emergency Services:

- Dial 112 for emergencies in Greece, connecting you to police, medical, and fire services.
- For non-emergency medical assistance, contact Tourist Police at 171.

Travel Insurance:

- Secure comprehensive travel insurance covering medical expenses and emergency evacuation.

Vaccinations:

- Routine vaccinations are recommended; consult your healthcare provider for additional advice based on your health and travel history.

Safety Tips:

Safe Drinking Water:

- Tap water is generally safe, though bottled water may be preferred in remote areas.

Sun Safety:

- Enjoy the sun responsibly with sunscreen, hats, and hydration, especially during peak hours.

Mosquito Protection:

- Combat mosquitoes with repellent, particularly during evenings.

Local Customs:

- Respect local customs for positive interactions with the community.

Emergency Contacts:

- Medical Emergency: Dial 112
- Tourist Police: Dial 171
- Corfu General Hospital: +30 26610 88200

COVID-19 Considerations:

- Stay informed about specific COVID-19 guidelines and follow local health advisories.

Safe Exploration:

- Practice common travel safety measures and safeguard valuables, especially in crowded areas.

Local Cuisine:

- Delight in local cuisine from reputable establishments, particularly for seafood.

Footwear for Exploration:

- Wear comfortable footwear for uneven terrain in historical sites and villages.

Emergency Exit Routes:

- Familiarize yourself with exit routes at your accommodation for emergency situations.

Corfu welcomes you with a commitment to tourism and essential services, ensuring a safe and enjoyable experience on this beautiful island.

Conclusion

distinctive encounters and enduring recollections awaiting you. Corfu, steeped in history, alive with culture, and adorned with breathtaking landscapes, has undoubtedly etched an unforgettable chapter in your travel saga.

Diverse Experiences:

From the historical marvels of Corfu Town to the tranquil allure of Paleokastritsa, every nook of the island unveils a spectrum of experiences. The crystalline waters of the beaches, the geniality of local hospitality, and the aromas of authentic cuisine weave together a tapestry of moments that linger in the heart.

Unveiling Secrets:

Corfu beckons you to uncover its hidden treasures, explore quaint villages, and embrace the lively ambiance of its cities. Whether traversing scenic trails, partaking in coastal water activities, or engaging in cultural revelries, each stride transforms into a new revelation.

Your Corfu Expedition:

As you commence your Corfu adventure, remember to not only capture the island's essence in photographs but also in the connections forged with locals. The amalgamation of ancient history and contemporary allure creates a distinctive atmosphere fostering exploration and contemplation.

Share Your Narratives:

Corfu isn't just a destination; it extends an invitation to craft your own tales. Share your experiences, the moments that stirred your spirit, and the serendipitous encounters that made your journey exceptional. Your narratives contribute to the collective chronicle that renders Corfu a timeless haven.

Maintain Connections:

Forge connections with fellow wanderers, exchange insights, and keep the discourse alive about the marvels of Corfu. The true beauty of travel lies not solely in the places visited but in the bonds formed and the tales carried forward.

Until We Reunite:

As you bid adieu to Corfu, carry with you the echoes of its history, the tastes of its cuisine, and the warmth of its people. Whether it be a return voyage or a cherished memory, Corfu will always extend a warm embrace.

Gratitude:

Thank you for allowing this guide to accompany you on your Corfu odyssey. May your travels be filled with elation, revelation, and the enchantment that Corfu uniquely offers.

Until we meet again on the shores of this exceptional island, safe travels, and may your journey be as remarkable as the destination itself.

Kaló Taxídi! (Safe Journey!)

Printed in Great Britain
by Amazon